THE BATTLE AGAINST BOREDOM

THE ADVENTURES OF THE HORNED AVENGER & BLT

Adventure #2 - How to Draw Cartoon Animals

THE HORNED AVENGER™

Ben Adams   Ray Nelson   Doug Kelly

MY RHINO SENSES ARE TINGLING AGAIN, LITTLE BUDDY... VON BOREDOM MUST BE NEAR!

THE HORNED AVENGER

Story:
Ray Nelson
Ben Adams

Art Direction:
Ben Adams

Pencils & Inking:
Ben Adams
Angus MacLane
Ray Nelson
Douglas Kelly

Computer:
Ben Adams
Ray Nelson
Julie Hansen
Kyle Holveck
Aaron Peeples
Kari Rasmussen
Matt Adams
Brud Giles

Editing:
Brian Feltovich

Rhino Wrangler:
Mike McLane

Stunts:
Chris Nelson
Holly McLane

Email The Horned Avenger at:
avenger@flyingrhino.com

Flying Rhinoceros
P.O. Box 3989 Portland, Oregon 97208
www.flyingrhino.com

ISBN 1-59168-011-5
Library of Congress Control Number: 2002100000

5

> I WILL SUMMON ALL OF MY RHINO POWERS TO HELP TURN THIS POOR CREATURE BACK INTO A PROUD MEMBER OF THE ANIMAL KINGDOM.

GETTING STARTED

Here are some basic steps that the Horned Avenger and BLT suggest to get started cartooning:

1. **Get Comfortable** Make sure that you have the necessary space, materials, and lighting for drawing cartoons.

2. **Research** Before you start drawing, it is very important that you do some research. Go to the library or get on the Internet and study pictures of the animals you want to draw.

3. **Brainstorm** Pick up your pencil and make a list of the first four or five features that come to mind when you think of your animal. For example, if you are drawing an elephant, the four most memorable features might be a trunk, tusks, big floppy ears, and a gigantic body.

4. **Exaggerate** To turn your animal into a cartoon, exaggerate the notable features. If your animal has a long nose, draw a really, really, really long nose.

5. **Do Rough Sketches** Remember that you are not doing a finished illustration. Spend your early drawing time doing rough sketches. The sketching stage is for experimenting and choosing basic shapes and characteristics. Fill in the details after you do a bunch of rough sketches.

6. **Have Fun!** If you aren't having fun, you need to put your drawing supplies away and relax. Go back to your drawings when you feel rested and are ready to have fun again.

Horned Avenger Hint
Exaggeration is making something extreme. If it is small, don't just draw it small; draw it really, really small.

ZEBRAS

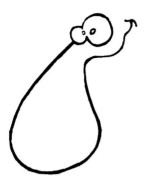

1. Start by drawing some cartoon eyes. Add a snout or nose. The snout starts under the eyes, droops down, and then curls back up into a silly grin.

2. Draw a circle around the eyes and mouth. Add nostrils by drawing two dots and putting an upside-down U over them. To make a goofy tongue, add a U to the bottom of the snout.

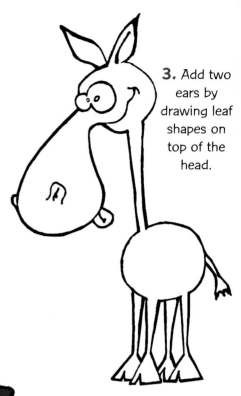

3. Add two ears by drawing leaf shapes on top of the head.

4. Draw two lines coming down from the head to make a great neck. The neck can be any length. Use a simple circle for the body, then add a tail. Draw legs in the same way you drew the neck

Use the basic body shape of the zebra to create other hoofed animals, such as cows, horses, camels, and giraffes.

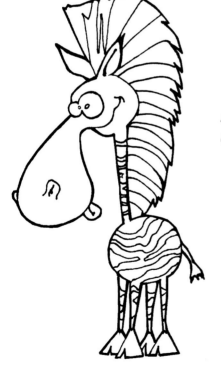

5. Draw the stripes and punk-rock mane. Hooves can be made by drawing a triangle with the flat edge at the bottom.

Try having your animal stand on its hind legs like a human.

Hoofed Animals

Camels

Make those humps big!

When people think of camels, they usually think of humps.

Giraffes

Giraffes are known for their long necks. Stretch those necks out as far as you can! Don't forget the silly little horns and all those spots.

Moose

Add huge antlers to the moose.

Horned Avenger Hint
To create movement, draw the legs sticking out of the front and back of the animal's body. Add a shadow underneath to make it look as if it's running.

Think tall, tall, tall!

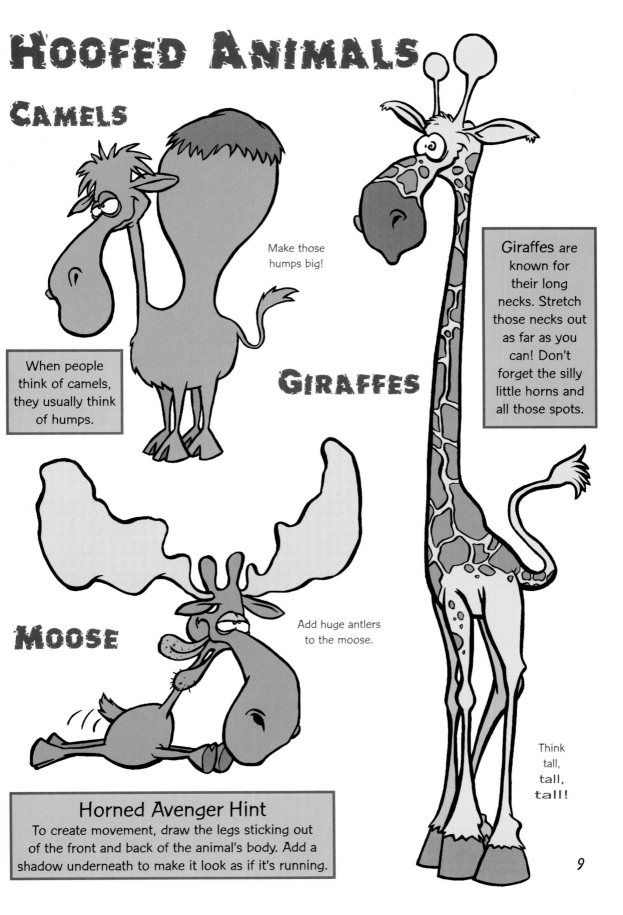

9

1. When drawing cats, start with the eyes. Any type of cartoon eyes will work.

2. Add a nose to your cat. An upside-down triangle (shaped like a piece of pizza) will work perfectly. Any size is fine.

3. On each side of the nose, add half circles. These pouches are for the whiskers.

upside-down letter U

letter U

4. Add some cheeks and a mouth. Notice that these pieces are just the letter U added to the nose and pouches.

5. Put some ears on his head. Again, use a U shape. Don't forget the whiskers.

Horned Avenger Hint

When you finish with the basic shapes, add details. For example, if you're drawing a lion, add a mane. If you're drawing a tiger, add stripes. You'll know what to add and where to put it if you research your animal.

IT HAS BECOME OBVIOUS THAT VON BOREDOM HAS WORKED HIS EVIL ON EVERY CREATURE IN THIS ZOO. THAT JUST TWISTS MY UNDIES IN A BUNCH.

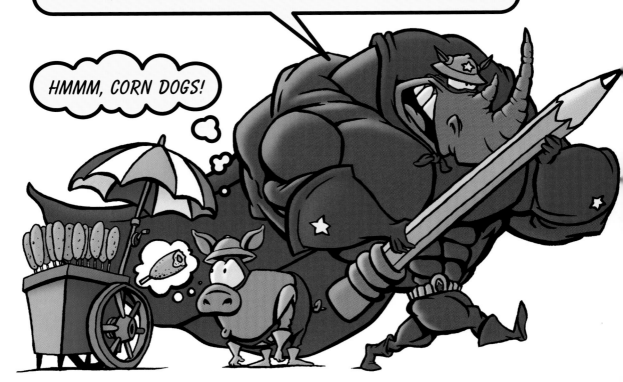

IT IS TIME FOR US TO GET TO WORK. WE MUST DRAW ALL OF THE ANIMALS BACK TO NORMAL. IF YOU DO YOUR RESEARCH, DRAW ROUGH SKETCHES, AND PRACTICE, PRACTICE, PRACTICE, YOU SHOULD SUCCEED! REMEMBER: NOT ALL OF YOUR DRAWINGS ARE GOING TO BE PERFECT RIGHT AWAY. YOU WILL DRAW SOME STINKERS. BUT DO NOT, I REPEAT, DO NOT GET DISCOURAGED! IF A DRAWING TURNS OUT BADLY, FIGURE OUT WHAT YOU DON'T LIKE ABOUT IT, THEN DRAW IT AGAIN. IT MAY TAKE 10, 20, OR EVEN 100 SKETCHES BEFORE IT LOOKS THE WAY YOU WANT IT TO LOOK. THE KEY IS TO STICK WITH IT.

HMMM, CORN DOGS!

Hippos

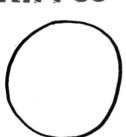

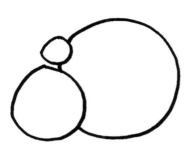

1. Start your hippo by drawing a big circle.

2. Add two smaller circles so that they overlap the big circle.

3. Connect the circles as shown. Add ears, eyes, nostrils, and big goofy teeth. Don't forget the tail.

4. To add legs, just draw little rectangles at the bottom of the big circle. Draw little upside-down U shapes for toenails.

If you want to turn your hippo into a rhino, add great big horns on the snout and erase the big, goofy teeth.

AHH, YOU ARE A STUNNING VISION! WAIT FOR ME, MY LITTLE TURTLEDOVE, AND I SHALL RETURN AFTER I DEFEAT THAT NASTY VON BOREDOM!

13

MONKEYS

oval #1

oval #2

1. Start with a circle.

2. Add eyes and three ovals.

oval #3

3. Add nostrils and lips. The lips should be added at the bottom of the nose oval and the nostrils added at the top.

4. Add rough edges to the oval shapes so they look as if they're covered with hair.

Monkeys have long, thin tails that act almost like extra arms.

Monkeys have long, skinny arms, legs, and bodies.

QUIT MONKEYING AROUND . . . WE NEED TO FIND VON BOREDOM.

14

APES

1. Start with an egg shape.

2. For eyes, draw two half circles under a straight line. Add two dots.

forehead wrinkles

nostrils

3. Draw a circle and place it under the egg shape.

punching bag

4. Create an open mouth. Then add a tongue and a little punching bag for the tonsils in the back of the throat. Make each ear with an upside-down letter U.

5. Add big, pointy teeth for a fierce-looking ape.

Apes also sport big, broad shoulders and big, round chest muscles.

BIG APE LOVE LITTLE PIG . . . GIVE BIG HUG AND LOTS OF KISSES!

WHAT ARE YOU? BANANAS? WAIT, LET ME REPHRASE THAT!

15

Gators

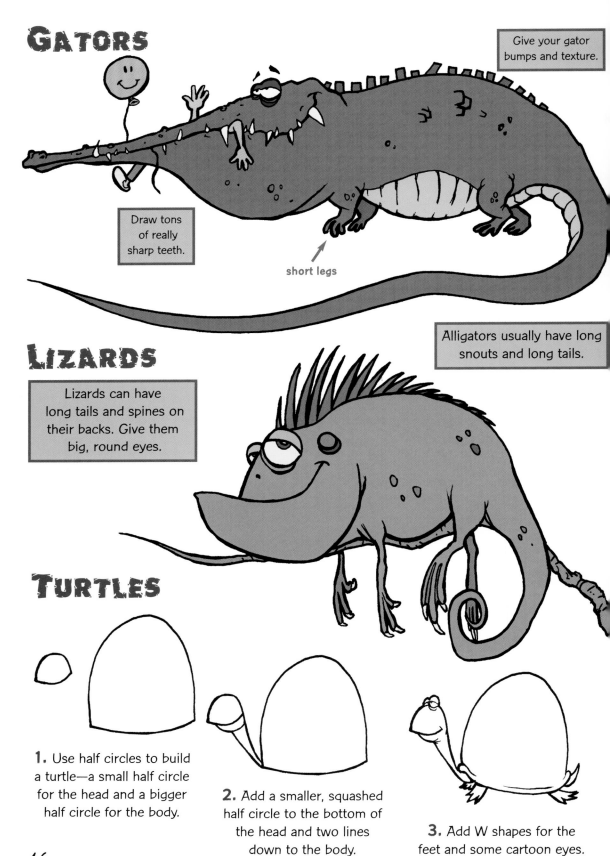

Give your gator bumps and texture.

Draw tons of really sharp teeth.

short legs

Lizards

Lizards can have long tails and spines on their backs. Give them big, round eyes.

Alligators usually have long snouts and long tails.

Turtles

1. Use half circles to build a turtle—a small half circle for the head and a bigger half circle for the body.

2. Add a smaller, squashed half circle to the bottom of the head and two lines down to the body.

3. Add W shapes for the feet and some cartoon eyes.

16

SNAKES

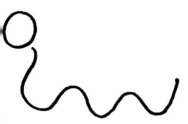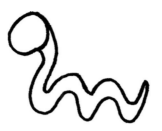

1. Snakes are very easy to draw. Start with a circle and a squiggly line.

2. Copy the shape of the squiggly line, joining the two lines at the tail. Then connect the lines to the circle.

3. Add two eyes on top of the circle. Draw a line across the circle for a mouth.

FROGS

1. To draw frogs, start with two big, round eyes. Add an oval for the body.

2. Draw a line across the oval to make a mouth.

3. Draw some legs. Frogs have long, webbed toes.

THE BARNYARD

SHEEP

Sheep can be drawn like other hoofed animals, but their bodies are a huge wad of wool with a head and four legs. (Start with the basic shapes that you learned on the hoofed animals page.) Have fun making different-sized sheep—tall, short, fat, and skinny.

"baa baa baa"

PIGS

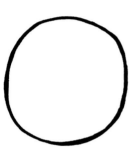   

1. Start with a circle and add another circle for a nose.

2. Add some eyes and a thin line for a mouth.

3. Pigs ears are shaped like leaves. Rectangles work for the legs.

4. You might try adding some human hands and feet and a curly tail.

Pigs are best known for their round snouts, curly tails, and big bellies. Just because a pig is usually round and fat doesn't mean you can't draw a skinny pig. Remember . . . **NO RULES!**

Cows

1. To build a cow, you'll need a snout, eyes, and nostrils.

2. Add some ears and horns. The horns can be any size you wish!

3. Make a neck by drawing two lines from the head. Then draw a fat rectangle to form the body.

4. Give the cow four legs and triangle-shaped hooves.

5. Add a tail and a tongue. Now, your bovine is ready to roll.

Try making your cow run or sit or even dance. The body size and shape may vary quite a bit. Don't be afraid to experiment. Cows can be different colors and patterns. Play around with different color combinations and spot designs.

Don't forget the udder on the cow.

19

Dogs

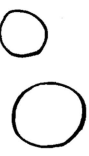

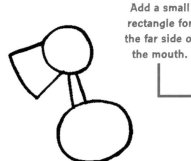

Add a small rectangle for the far side of the mouth.

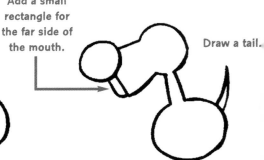

Draw a tail.

1. Start your dog with two circles.

2. On the top circle, add a rectangle shape extending outward. Connect the circles with two lines for a neck.

3. Add a smaller circle at the end of the rectangle for the nose.

4. Give your dog floppy ears and a tongue. Extend lines down from the body to create the legs.

5. Finish your dog by adding the eyes and feet. Feet are ovals that extend out from the legs. Add several little lines for toes.

For a poodle, try fluffy fur puffs all over your dog's body.

Do some research at the library or on the Internet to find different breeds of dogs to cartoon. Bulldogs have huge bottom jaws. Great Danes have big cheeks. Add a collar for character.

Great Dane

Bulldog

NO RULES!

Horned Avenger Hint
Don't be afraid to get weird with your characters.
Cartoons can do the unexpected. Have a
jack-in-the-box pop out of a kangaroo's
pouch or put a camel in a tuxedo.

RODENTS

Rabbit ears are big, big, big.

When drawing rabbits and rodents—such as mice, squirrels, and beavers—you can use the same face over and over again. For example, a mouse has basically the same face as a rabbit; however, the rabbit will have bigger feet and ears and a fuzzy tail.

RABBITS

A good nose shape is like a slice of pizza.

1. Start with a circle or oval.

2. Add some eyes and a nose.

3. Add an upside-down letter Y to the nose. Then draw two squares for the big, gnawing teeth.

4. Add some big, flat feet and a fluffy cotton tail.

RATS

A rat may have a long or short nose. Don't forget its long tail.

AW, LOOK AT ALL THE CUTE, CUDDLY, FUZZY RODENTS!

THE HORNED AVENGER FEARS NOTHING!

DON'T COME ANY CLOSER, RHINO BOY! I'M NOT AFRAID TO USE THESE RODENTS! HUNDREDS OF INNOCENT ZOO-GOERS MAY BE HURT!

YOU'RE BLUFFING, VON BOREDOM. EVEN YOU WOULDN'T RISK THE MASS DESTRUCTION CAUSED BY RANDOM RODENT FIRE!

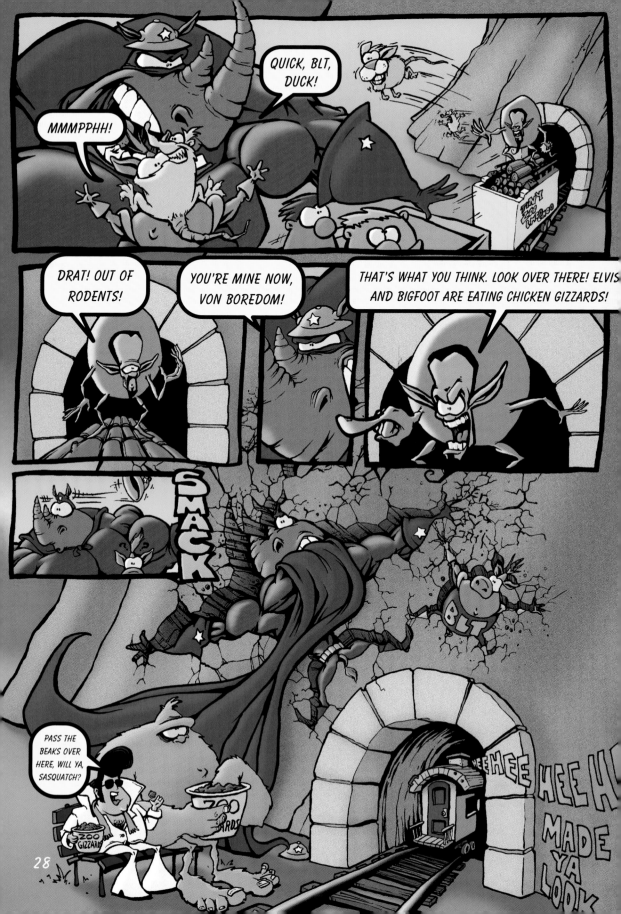

NOW, TO ESCAPE THAT GOOFY RHINO AND HIS PATHETIC PIG PAL FOR GOOD!

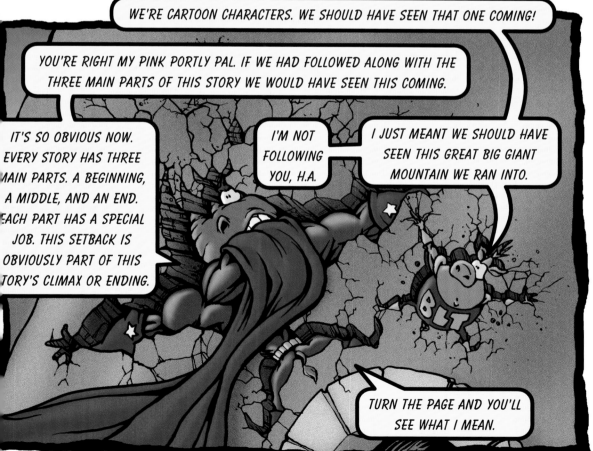

WE'RE CARTOON CHARACTERS. WE SHOULD HAVE SEEN THAT ONE COMING!

YOU'RE RIGHT MY PINK PORTLY PAL. IF WE HAD FOLLOWED ALONG WITH THE THREE MAIN PARTS OF THIS STORY WE WOULD HAVE SEEN THIS COMING.

IT'S SO OBVIOUS NOW. EVERY STORY HAS THREE MAIN PARTS. A BEGINNING, A MIDDLE, AND AN END. EACH PART HAS A SPECIAL JOB. THIS SETBACK IS OBVIOUSLY PART OF THIS STORY'S CLIMAX OR ENDING.

I'M NOT FOLLOWING YOU, H.A.

I JUST MEANT WE SHOULD HAVE SEEN THIS GREAT BIG GIANT MOUNTAIN WE RAN INTO.

TURN THE PAGE AND YOU'LL SEE WHAT I MEAN.

BEGINNING

THE BEGINNING OF ANY GOOD STORY IS WHERE THE READER OR VIEWER LEARNS ALL ABOUT THE SETTING AND CHARACTERS. THE BEGINNING IS ALSO WHERE THE PLOT IS INTRODUCED.

EVERYTHING HAS TO HAPPEN SOMEWHERE. BECAUSE IF SOMETHING HAPPENS NOWHERE, IT'S NOTHING, RIGHT? WAIT...BEFORE OUR BRAINS SEIZE UP, LET'S TRY TO SAY THAT A DIFFERENT WAY. WHEN YOU'RE DEVELOPING A CARTOON STORY, THINK OF DIFFERENT SETTINGS AND THE POSSIBILITIES THEY OFFER.

THINK OF THE AMAZING STORY POSSIBILITIES SUGGESTED BY THESE SETTINGS:
- ▶ A ROCKET LAUNCHING PAD, 90 SECONDS BEFORE LIFTOFF
- ▶ A DOGSLED RACE THROUGH FROZEN ALASKA
- ▶ A LIFEBOAT IN THE MIDDLE OF A STORMY OCEAN

ONCE YOU'VE PICKED A PLACE FOR THINGS TO HAPPEN, YOU NEED SOME CHARACTERS FOR THINGS TO HAPPEN TO. CHARACTERS HELP DRAW YOUR READER INTO THE STORY. INCLUDE A CHARACTER THAT READERS WILL LIKE AND ROOT FOR...LIKE ME...AND A CHARACTER THAT READERS WILL DISLIKE AND WANT TO BOO ON SIGHT...BARON VON BOREDOM, FOR EXAMPLE. IT'S ALSO A GOOD IDEA TO BRING FUNNY CHARACTERS INTO YOUR STORY FOR COMIC RELIEF.

WHY DON'T WE HAVE ANY FUNNY CHARACTERS, AVENGER?

OH, IF YOU ONLY KNEW, MY FUNNY LITTLE FRIEND. (PAUSE) THESE ARE JUST SOME IDEAS. TRY YOUR OWN COMBINATIONS OF CHARACTERS: MEN AND WOMEN, OLD PEOPLE AND BABIES, FLYING DOGS AND FLYING CATS.

RISING ACTION

INTRODUCTION

Horned Avenge Hint

Let brainstorms reign
Spend some time every
thinking up far-out settir
interesting characters, a
especially crazy story ide
Then write 'em down

CLIMAX

MIDDLE

THE *MIDDLE* OF A STORY IS WHERE PLOT AND CONFLICT BECOME IMPORTANT. YOU'VE GOT A GREAT SETTING THAT PROVIDES YOU WITH LOTS OF INTERESTING STORY POSSIBILITIES. YOU'VE GOT CHARACTERS WHO WILL INVOLVE READERS IN YOUR STORY. NOW, WHAT'S GOING TO HAPPEN IN YOUR STORY? YOU NEED A WAY TO STRUCTURE ALL THE GREAT STORY IDEAS YOU HAVE IN YOUR HEAD. THE *PLOT* IS THE EVENTS YOU DREAMED UP, LINKED TOGETHER TO TELL A STORY..

EVERY PLOT NEEDS A *PROBLEM*, OR *CONFLICT*. THIS DOESN'T MEAN THERE HAS TO BE A WAR OR EVEN A PILLOW FIGHT. IT ONLY MEANS THAT SOMEONE IN THE STORY HAS TO WANT SOMETHING. IN OUR CASE WE WANT TO CAPTURE BARON VON BOREDOM SO HE WILL NOT BE ABLE TO END CREATIVITY.

THE *RISING ACTION* IS THE SERIES OF EVENTS THAT BUILD UP TO A CLIMAX. THE PROBLEM, OR CONFLICT, GETS MORE SERIOUS, OFTEN BECAUSE OF *COMPLICATIONS*. THE AUDIENCE IS KEPT IN SUSPENSE WHILE THEY WAIT TO SEE IF THE CONFLICT CAN BE RESOLVED. WE ARE AT THE CLIMAX PART OF OUR STORY RIGHT NOW. IF WE HAD BEEN FOLLOWING THE STRUCTURE OF THIS STORY, WE PROBABLY WOULD HAVE KNOWN SOMETHING LIKE THIS MOUNTAIN WAS GOING TO COME ALONG.

RESOLUTION

END

THE *END* OF THE STORY IS WHERE OUR CONFLICT IS SOLVED.

THE *CLIMAX* IS THE PLACE IN THE STORY WHERE EVERYTHING CHANGES. THE ORIGINAL PROBLEM IS SOLVED; THE CONFLICT ENDS.

EVEN AFTER THE MAIN PROBLEM IS SOLVED, THERE ARE PROBABLY STILL SOME LOOSE ENDS TO TIE UP. DURING THE *RESOLUTION*, YOU CAN CLEAR UP ALL THE COMPLICATIONS THAT YOU INTRODUCED DURING THE RISING ACTION. YOU CAN ALSO SHOW HOW THE CLIMAX AFFECTS VARIOUS CHARACTERS IN THE STORY.

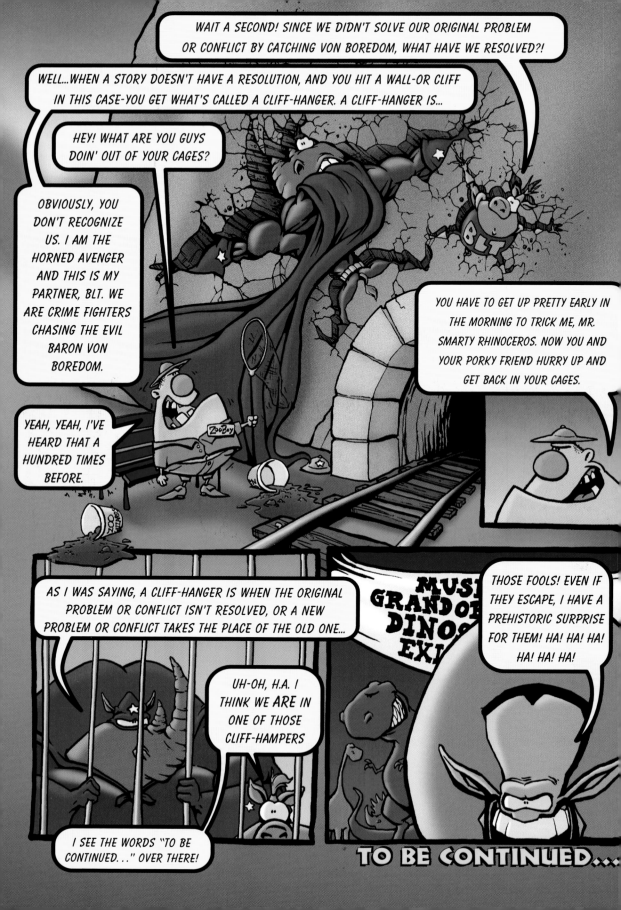